THE KINGFISHER
First Picture Atlas

Written by Deborah Chancellor

Illustrated by Anthony Lewis

KINGFISHER

BOSTON

KINGFISHER

a Houghton Mifflin Company imprint
222 Berkeley Street
Boston, Massachusetts 02116
www.houghtonmifflinbooks.com

Author: Deborah Chancellor
Senior editor: Belinda Weber
Coordinating editor: Stephanie Pliakas
Art director: Mike Davis
Consultant: Keith Lye
DTP manager: Nicky Studdart
DTP operator: Primrose Burton
Senior production controller: Lindsey Scott
Picture research manager: Cee Weston-Baker
Proofreader: Sheila Clewley
Cover design: Mike Davis, Jane Tassie
Illustrations: Anthony Lewis

First published in 2005
First published in this format in 2007

10 9 8 7 6 5 4 3 2 1
1TR/0307/SHENS/CLSN(CLSN)/158MA/C

Copyright © Kingfisher
Publications Plc 2005

LIBRARY OF CONGRESS CATALOGING-IN-
PUBLICATION DATA has been applied for.

ISBN 978-0-7534-5941-6

Printed in Taiwan

Contents

CREDITS
The publisher would like to thank the following for permission
to reproduce their material. Every care has been taken to trace copyright
holders. However, if there have been unintentional omissions or failure to
trace copyright holders, we apologize and will, if informed, endeavor to
make corrections in any future edition.

2 NASA; 7 Corbis/Galen Rowell; 8 Corbis/Yann Arthus-Bertrand; 13
Photolibrary/Walter Bibikow; 15 Alamy/Robert Harding Picture Library;
16 Alamy/Bob Turner; 19 Alamy/ Robert Harding Picture Library; 20
Alamy/Imagestate; 22 Alamy/Andre Jenny; 24 Alamy/Mervyn Rees; 27
Corbis/ Reuters; 28 Getty/311214-001; 30 Corbis/Arko Datta/Reuters;
32 Alamy/SC Photos; 35 Alamy/Worldwide Pic Lib; 37 Photolibrary/John
Downer; 38 Corbis/Yann Arthus-Bertrand; 41 Alamy/Robert Harding
Picture Library; 42 Rex; 43 Getty/Stone; 45 Alamy/Nordicphotos

About Earth

Earth is a planet in space. It is shaped like a ball and is covered with land and water. Photographs can show us what Earth looks like. Maps help us understand more about the world.

Countries of the world

A country, such as Italy (map above), is a part of the world with its own people and laws. There are around 200 countries in the world. This number changes if countries break up or join together in new ways.

Continents

A continent is a huge
area of land. Some continents,
such as South America (map
above), contain many different
countries. On maps of continents
lines are drawn to show the
borders between countries.
You cannot see these lines
on a photograph because
they are not really there.

What is a map?

A map is a picture of Earth that shows natural and human-made features. A globe is a type of map that is made in the shape of a ball, just like Earth itself. We cannot see the whole world at once on a globe. If we want to do this, we need to look at a flat map.

Making a map

To make a flat map, the globe is split into segments and then "peeled" like an orange.

The segments are then placed side by side.

These segments are used to create a flat map (see the map of the world on page 10).

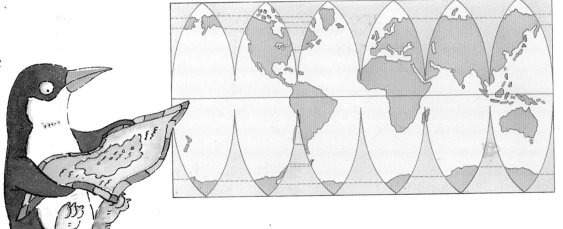

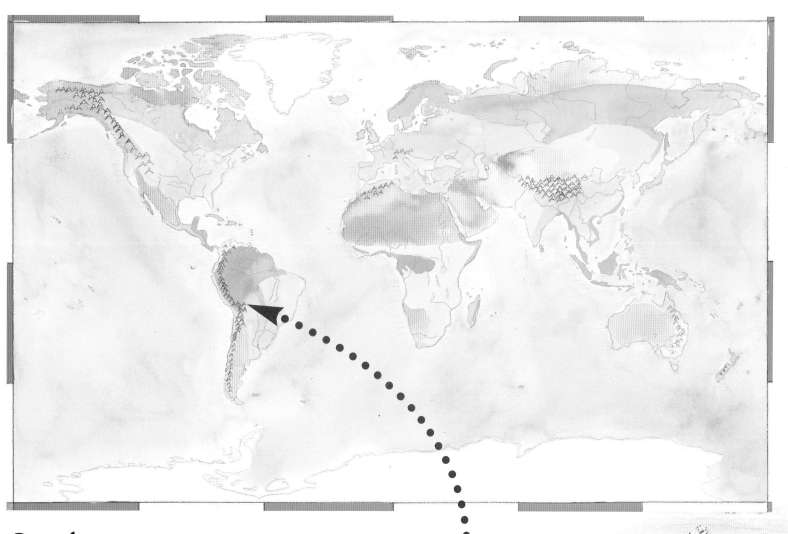

On the map

Most maps show the curved surface of Earth on a flat piece of paper. Mapmakers have to change the shape of some countries and oceans in order to fit them together on a flat map.

Showing mountains

Special colors and symbols on maps show us where to find important features of the landscape—such as these beautiful mountains in South America.

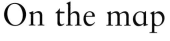

Using an atlas

An atlas is a book of maps. To use an atlas, you need to understand how maps work. Maps are much smaller than the places that they show. They have a lot of information in a very small space.

Pictures show industries, animals, or landmarks.

Grid band "C"

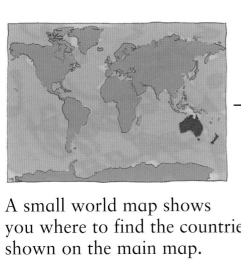

A small world map shows you where to find the countries shown on the main map.

Grid band "2"

A grid helps you find places on the map. Here, Alice Springs is in square C2. You can find this by tracing your finger down from the letter C band and across from the number 2 band.

In this atlas a story box focuses on an interesting fact.

| A | B | C |

Darwin

Seahorses

Gulf Carpent

Abbriginal cave paintings

NORTHERN TERRITORY

Great Sandy Desert

AUSTRAL

TROPIC OF CAPRICORN

Mining

Alice Springs

Simpson Desert

Gibson Desert

WESTERN AUSTRALIA

SOUTH AUSTRALI

Lake

Kangaroos

The Ghan

Great Victoria Desert

Perth

Farming

Adelaide

Great Australian Bight

Great white sharks

Uluru (Ayers Rock) is a sandstone monolith rising high up above the desert in Australia's Northern Territory. It is the largest rock of that type in the world. **Look for the blue star**

38

| A | B | C |

8

Map key

Colors, lines, and symbols on maps stand for many different things. These details are explained in a key to the map. In this atlas the key helps you find cities, borders, and rivers. It also explains what the colors on the map mean.

KEY

■ capital city ⌒ country border

● city - - - state border

• town - ·- · disputed border

▲ highest point

river   lake

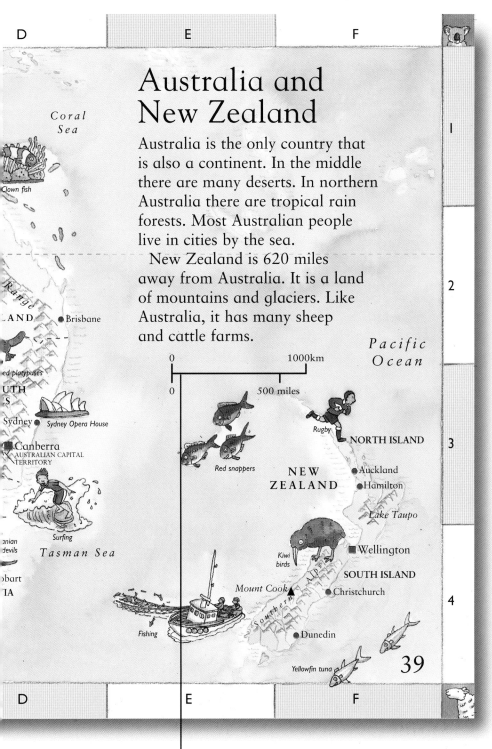

Australia and New Zealand

Australia is the only country that is also a continent. In the middle there are many deserts. In northern Australia there are tropical rain forests. Most Australian people live in cities by the sea.

New Zealand is 620 miles away from Australia. It is a land of mountains and glaciers. Like Australia, it has many sheep and cattle farms.

Coral Sea

Clown fish

Brisbane

ed platypuses

Sydney Sydney Opera House

Canberra
AUSTRALIAN CAPITAL
TERRITORY

Surfing

anian devils

Tasman Sea

bart

Pacific Ocean

Rugby

NORTH ISLAND

Red snappers

NEW ZEALAND

Auckland

Hamilton

Lake Taupo

Kiwi birds

Wellington

SOUTH ISLAND

Mount Cook ▲

Christchurch

Fishing

Dunedin

Yellowfin tuna

39

0 _____ 1000km
0 _____ 500 miles

Desert Dry area with few plants, often with sand and rocks

Dry grassland Flat, grassy plains with only a few trees

Temperate grassland Flat, grassy plains with some trees

Forest Area with many trees

Mountains Tall hills and rugged land

Tundra Flat area close to the Arctic with frozen ground and no trees

Ice and snow Place where ice and snow covers the ground

Seas and oceans Salty water that covers most of Earth

A scale bar helps you understand how big areas are on the map.

9

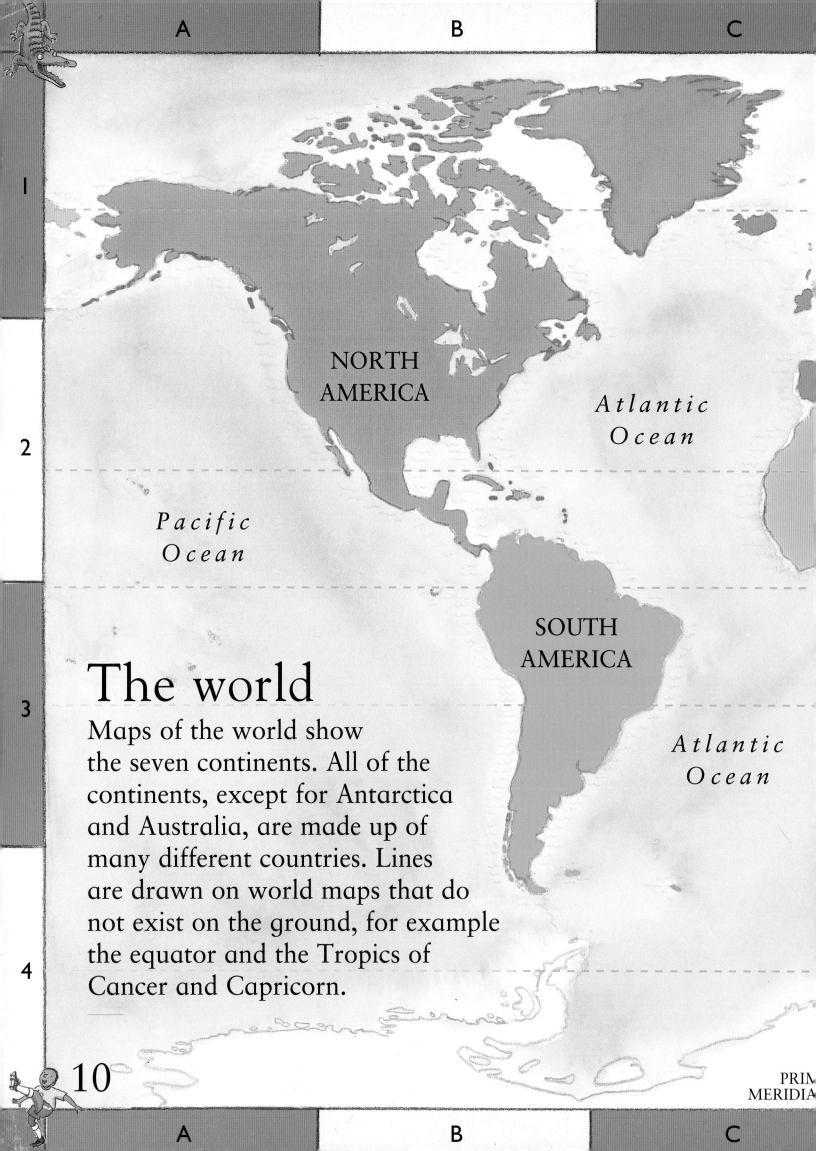

1

NORTH
AMERICA

*Atlantic
Ocean*

2

*Pacific
Ocean*

SOUTH
AMERICA

3

The world

Maps of the world show
the seven continents. All of the
continents, except for Antarctica
and Australia, are made up of
many different countries. Lines
are drawn on world maps that do
not exist on the ground, for example
the equator and the Tropics of
Cancer and Capricorn.

*Atlantic
Ocean*

4

10

PRIM
MERIDIA

rctic Ocean

ROPE

ASIA

RICA

ARCTIC CIRCLE

Pacific Ocean

TROPIC OF CANCER

EQUATOR

Indian Ocean

TROPIC OF CAPRICORN

AUSTRALIA

Southern Ocean

ANTARCTIC CIRCLE

ANTARCTICA

1

2

3

4

11

Canada and Alaska

Canada is a huge country with the longest coastline in the world. Most Canadians live in towns and cities in the south. Canada and Alaska are in the continent of North America. Alaska is not actually a country—it is one of the 50 U.S. states.

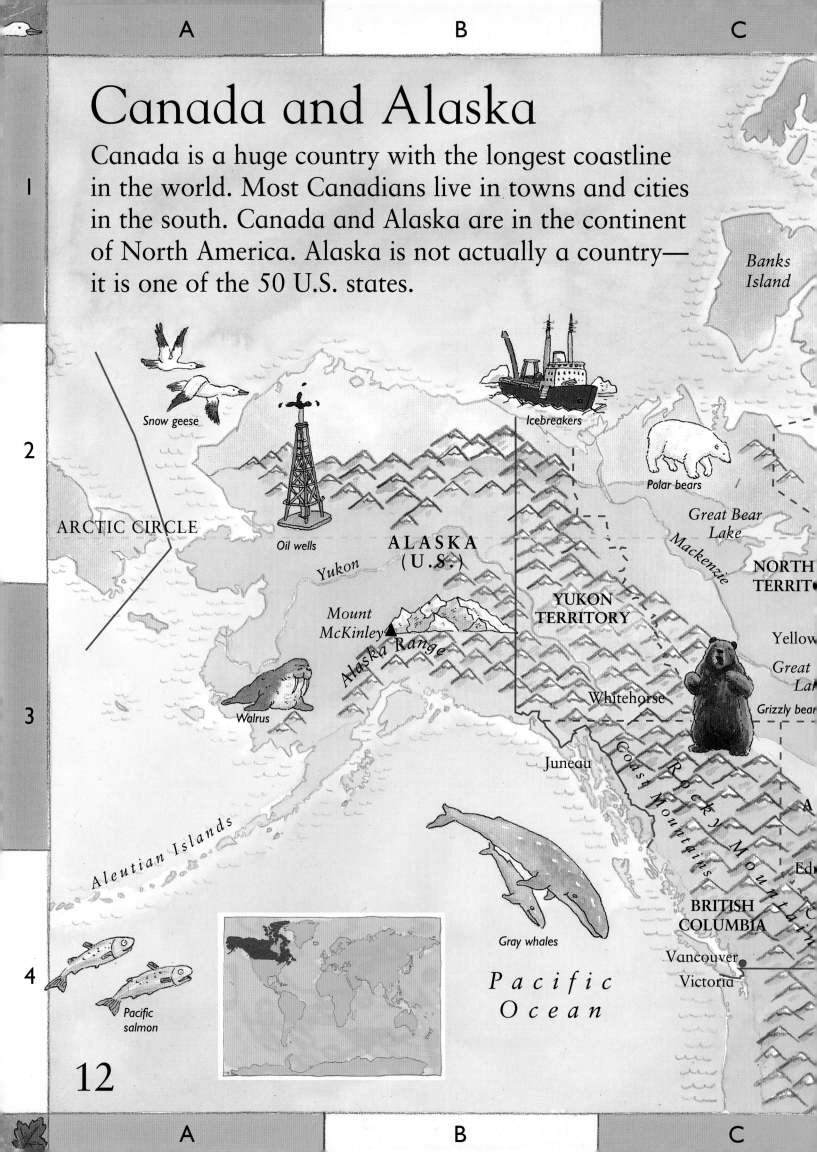

Snow geese

Icebreakers

Banks Island

Oil wells

ARCTIC CIRCLE

Polar bears

ALASKA (U.S.)

Great Bear Lake

Mackenzie

NORTH TERRITO

Yukon

Mount McKinley

Alaska Range

YUKON TERRITORY

Yellow

Great La

Walrus

Whitehorse

Grizzly bear

Juneau

Rocky Mountains

Coast Mountains

Aleutian Islands

A

Ed

Gray whales

BRITISH COLUMBIA

Pacific Ocean

Vancouver

Victoria

Pacific salmon

12

D   E   F

Elizabeth Islands

Ellesmere Island

Devon Island

Québec City is the only walled city in North America. It was founded in 1608 and is almost 400 years old.

Look for the blue star ✦

Victoria Island

Baffin Island

NUNAVUT

ARCTIC CIRCLE

Reindeer

Inuit people

Iqaluit

Lake Athabasca

H u d s o n B a y

Icebergs

MANITOBA

SASKATCHEWAN

C A N A D A

Lake Winnipeg

Timber industry

ONTARIO

A t l a n t i c O c e a n

Skiing

QUÉBEC

NEWFOUNDLAND AND LABRADOR

Manufacturing

St. Lawrence

PRINCE EDWARD ISLAND

Farming
Regina

Winnipeg

CN Tower

Lake Superior

NEW BRUNSWICK

St. John's

Charlottetown

1000km

Québec

Montreal

Fredericton

1

2

3

4

Lake Huron

Lake Michigan

Toronto

Ottawa

Lake Ontario

Halifax

NOVA SCOTIA

500 miles

Lake Erie

13

I

2

3

4

HAWAII

Honolulu

Pacific Ocean

WASHINGTON

Seattle

Space Needle

Olympia

Salem

Cascade Range

Timber industry

OREGON

Boise

IDAHO

Helena

Cattle ranching

MONTAN[A]

Ru

WYOMIN[G]

Raccoons

Great Salt Lake

Salt Lake City

Che

Pacific Ocean

NEVADA

Sacramento

Carson City

UTAH

Colorado

COLO[RADO]

D

San Francisco

CALIFORNIA

Rattlesnakes

Cacti

S

Movie industry

Los Angeles

San Diego

ARIZONA

Phoenix

The United States of America

The U.S. has 50 states, including Alaska (see the map on pages 12–13) and Hawaii. People from all over the world have settled there, but the first to live there were the Native Americans. Most of the people now live in cities along the east coast.

14

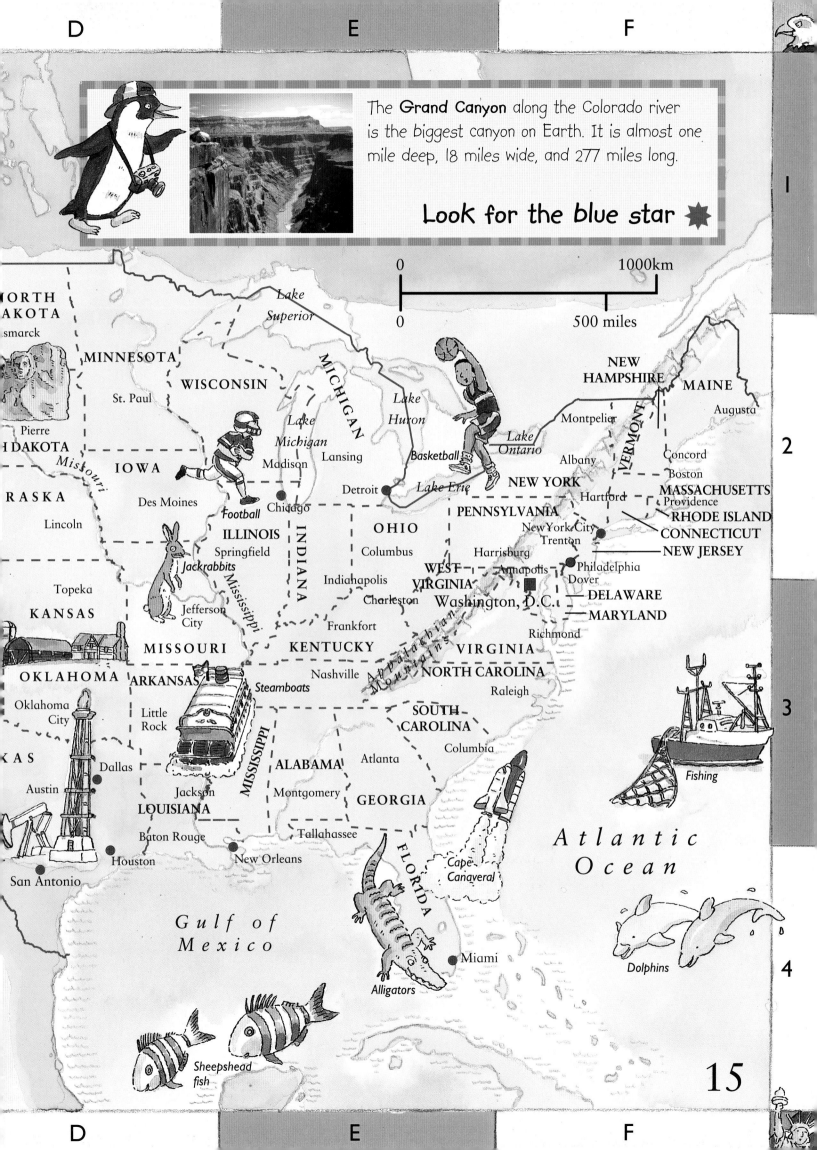

The **Grand Canyon** along the Colorado river is the biggest canyon on Earth. It is almost one mile deep, 18 miles wide, and 277 miles long.

Look for the blue star ✦

0   1000km

0   500 miles

NORTH DAKOTA
Bismarck

MINNESOTA

Lake Superior

NEW HAMPSHIRE

MAINE
Augusta

WISCONSIN
St. Paul

MICHIGAN

Lake Huron

Montpelier

Pierre

SOUTH DAKOTA

Lake Michigan

Lansing

Lake Ontario

Albany

VERMONT

Concord
Boston

Missouri

IOWA

Madison

Basketball

NEW YORK

Hartford

MASSACHUSETTS
Providence

NEBRASKA

Des Moines

Chicago

Detroit

Lake Erie

PENNSYLVANIA

New York City
Trenton

RHODE ISLAND
CONNECTICUT
NEW JERSEY

Lincoln

Football

ILLINOIS
Springfield

INDIANA

OHIO
Columbus

Harrisburg

Philadelphia
Dover

Topeka

Jackrabbits

Mississippi

Indianapolis

WEST VIRGINIA

Annapolis

DELAWARE

KANSAS

Jefferson City

Charleston

Washington, D.C.

MARYLAND

OKLAHOMA

MISSOURI

KENTUCKY

Frankfort

Richmond

VIRGINIA

Oklahoma City

ARKANSAS

Nashville

Appalachian Mountains

NORTH CAROLINA

Steamboats

Raleigh

TEXAS

Little Rock

SOUTH CAROLINA

Dallas

MISSISSIPPI

Columbia

Austin

Jackson

ALABAMA

Atlanta

Fishing

LOUISIANA

Montgomery

GEORGIA

Baton Rouge

Tallahassee

San Antonio

Houston

New Orleans

FLORIDA

Cape Canaveral

Atlantic Ocean

Gulf of Mexico

Alligators

Miami

Dolphins

Sheepshead fish

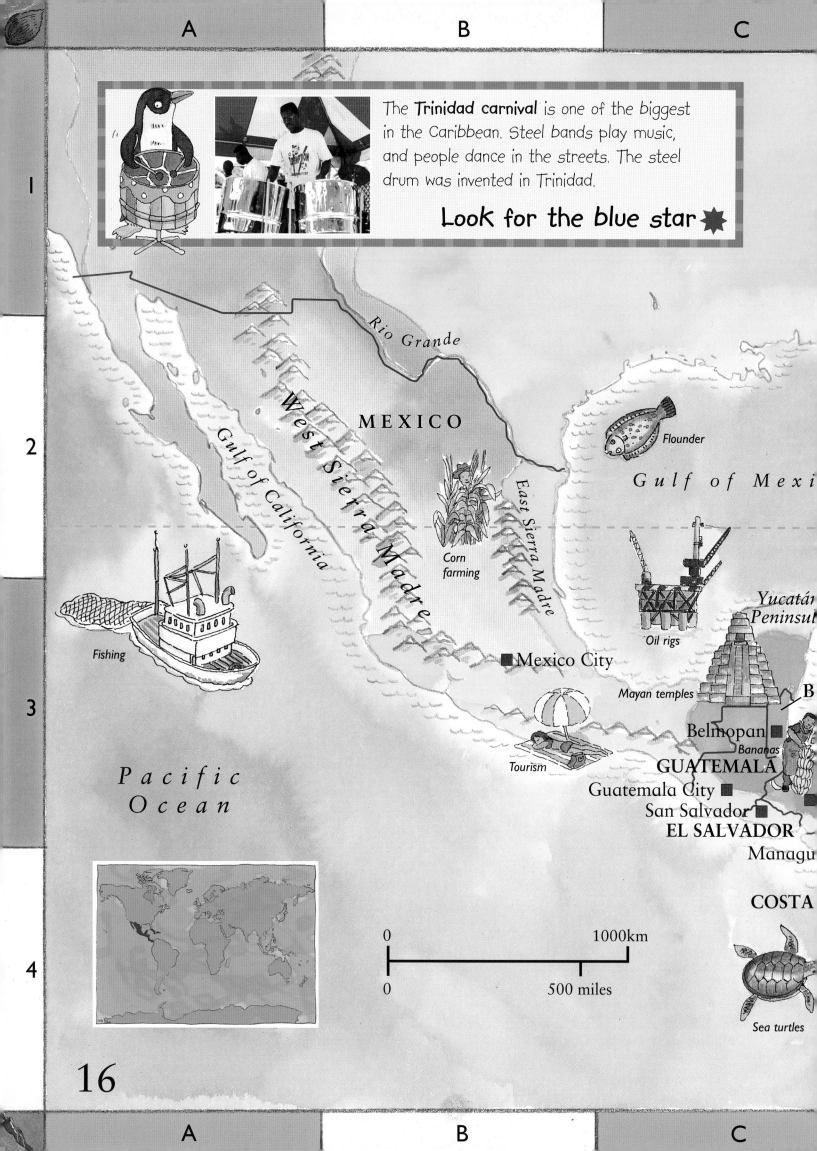

I

The **Trinidad carnival** is one of the biggest in the Caribbean. Steel bands play music, and people dance in the streets. The steel drum was invented in Trinidad.

Look for the blue star ✴

Rio Grande

MEXICO

West Sierra Madre

Gulf of California

Flounder

2

Gulf of Mexi

East Sierra Madre

Corn farming

Oil rigs

Yucatán Peninsul

■ Mexico City

Mayan temples

Belmopan ■
Bananas
GUATEMALA

Guatemala City ■

Fishing

Pacific Ocean

Tourism

3

San Salvador ■
EL SALVADOR

Managu

COSTA

B

0 —————————————— 1000km

0 —————————————— 500 miles

4

Sea turtles

Mexico, Central America, and the Caribbean

Mexico, Central America, and the Caribbean islands are in the continent of North America. Mexico is the largest country in the region. The islands of the Caribbean are countries, too. More than half of all Caribbean people live in Cuba and the Dominican Republic.

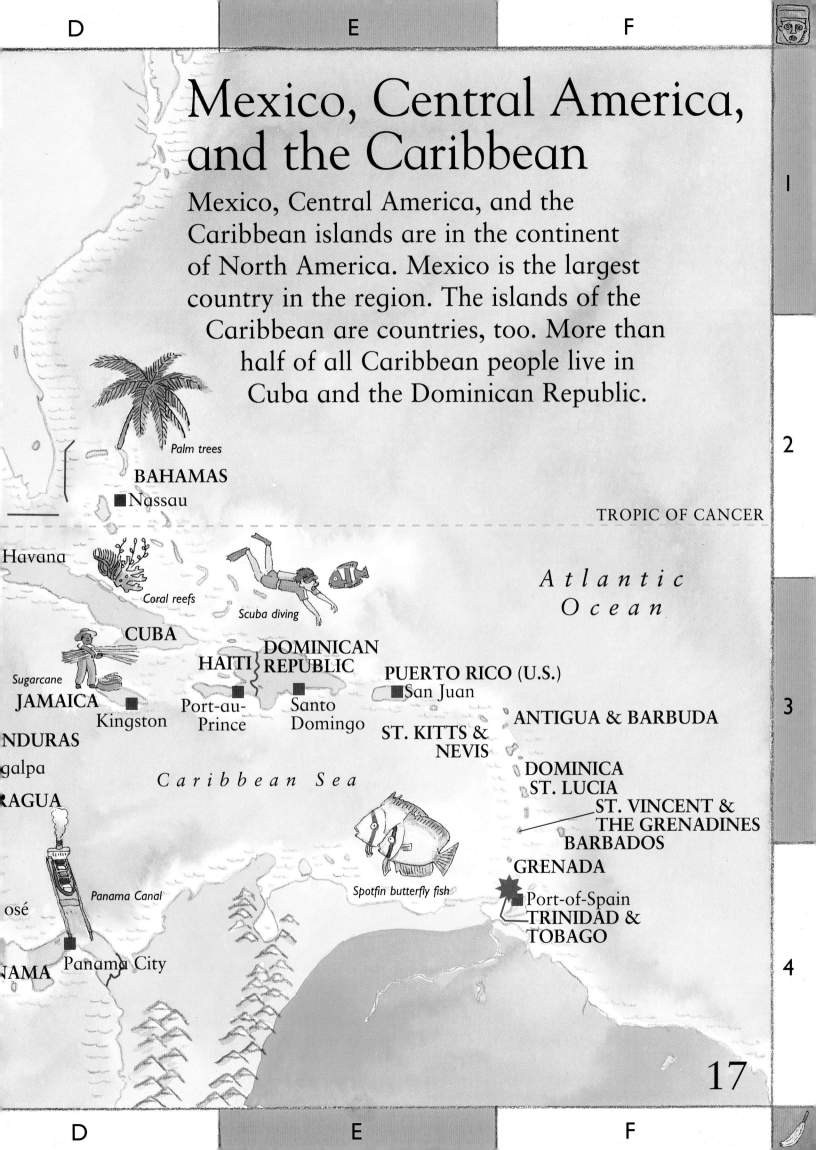

Palm trees

BAHAMAS
■ Nassau

TROPIC OF CANCER

Havana

Coral reefs

Scuba diving

A t l a n t i c   O c e a n

Sugarcane

CUBA

DOMINICAN REPUBLIC

HAITI

PUERTO RICO (U.S.)
■ San Juan

JAMAICA ■

Port-au-Prince

Santo Domingo

ANTIGUA & BARBUDA

Kingston

ST. KITTS & NEVIS

NDURAS

galpa

C a r i b b e a n   S e a

DOMINICA
ST. LUCIA

RAGUA

ST. VINCENT & THE GRENADINES
BARBADOS

GRENADA

Spotfin butterfly fish

osé

Panama Canal

■ Port-of-Spain
TRINIDAD & TOBAGO

JAMA Panama City

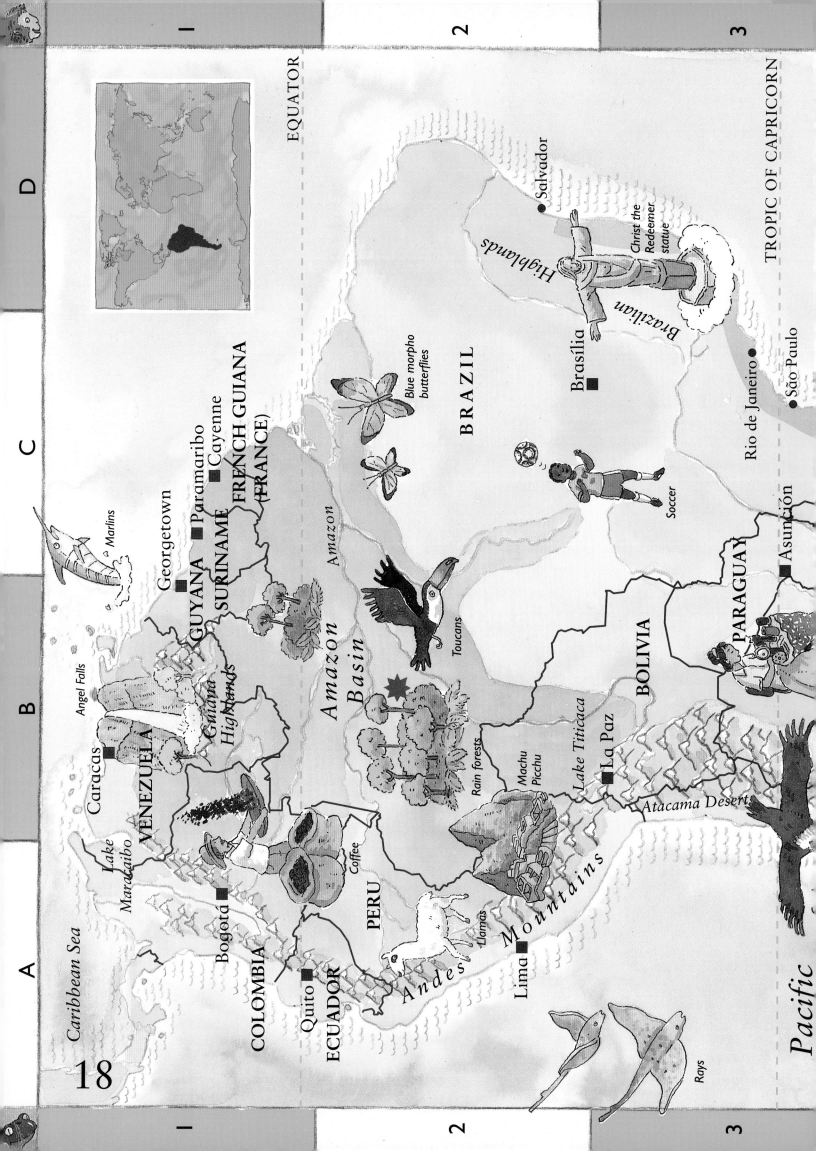

18

EQUATOR

TROPIC OF CAPRICORN

Caribbean Sea

Marlins

Lake Maracaibo

Angel Falls

Caracas ■

VENEZUELA

Bogotá ■

COLOMBIA

Quito ■

ECUADOR

Georgetown ■

GUYANA

Paramaribo ■

SURINAME

Cayenne ■

**FRENCH GUIANA
(FRANCE)**

*Guiana
Highlands*

Coffee

PERU

Lima ■

Rain forests

Machu Picchu

Llamas

Amazon

Amazon Basin

Blue morpho butterflies

Toucans

Brazilian Highlands

B R A Z I L

Salvador ●

Brasília ■

Christ the Redeemer statue

Soccer

Rio de Janeiro ●

São Paulo ●

Lake Titicaca

La Paz ■

BOLIVIA

Atacama Desert

Andes Mountains

PARAGUAY

Asunción ■

Rays

Pacific

South America

South America is a continent of extremes. Tall, snowy mountains lie in the west, while the steamy Amazon rain forest covers a huge area in the north. The southern tip of the continent is very dry and freezing cold.

The Amazon rain forest contains around half of all of the animal and plant species in the world. Many more are still waiting to be discovered.

Look for the blue star

0   500 miles
0   1000km

Airplanes

URUGUAY
■ Montevideo

Paraná

■ Buenos Aires

ARGENTINA

Sheep farming

FALKLAND ISLANDS (U.K.)
■ Stanley

Oil rigs

Santiago ■

Andes Mou

Grapes

Concepción ●

CHILE

Patagonia

Cape Horn

Sardines

Fishing

A   B   C   D

Northern Europe

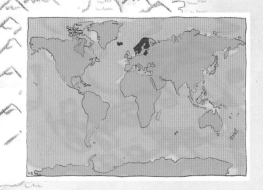

Forests, lakes, and mountains cover large parts of northern Europe. The countries of Norway, Sweden, and Denmark make up a region called Scandinavia. To the east is Finland. South of the Baltic Sea are the small countries of Estonia, Latvia, and Lithuania.

ARCTIC CIRCLE

ICELAND

Geysers
■ Reykjavik

Cod

Iceland cat sharks

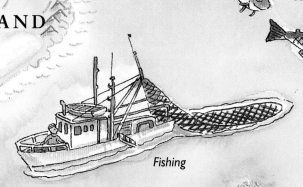

Fishing

*A t l a n t i c
O c e a n*

Hans Christian Andersen, a famous children's book writer, lived in Denmark. A statue of his "Little Mermaid" is in Copenhagen, the capital city of Denmark.

Look for the blue star ✶

N

20

I

400km

200 miles

Hammerfest

L a p l a n d

Fjords

Kiruna

Arctic foxes

ARCTIC CIRCLE

Fishing

Reindeer and Sami people

Pine forests

2

Norwegian Sea

FINLAND

Oulu

Lake Oulujärvi

SWEDEN

Paper mills

Trondheim

igs

Pine forests

Gulf of Bothnia

L a k e Region

3

en

Åland

Helsinki

Gulf of Finland

NORWAY

Manufacturing

Baltic Sea

Tallinn

Oslo

Stockholm

ESTONIA

Lake Vänern

Lake Vättern

Göteborg

Gotland

LATVIA

Ríga

4

DENMARK

Pig farming

Cattle farming

Copenhagen

LITHUANIA

Lego toys

Vilnius

21

Western Europe

Most of the land in western Europe is used for farming. Industries, such as car factories, are also important. Some cities are very old and attract many tourists. Countries around the Mediterranean Sea are very hot in the summer.

Atlantic Ocean

Puffins

Cod

Oil rigs

North Sea

Windmills

Tulips

Car factories

Baltic Sea

Edinburgh

SCOTLAND

UNITED KINGDOM

NORTHERN IRELAND

Belfast

Dublin

Computers

France's most famous landmark, the **Eiffel Tower,** sways up to five inches from side to side in high winds.

Look for the blue star

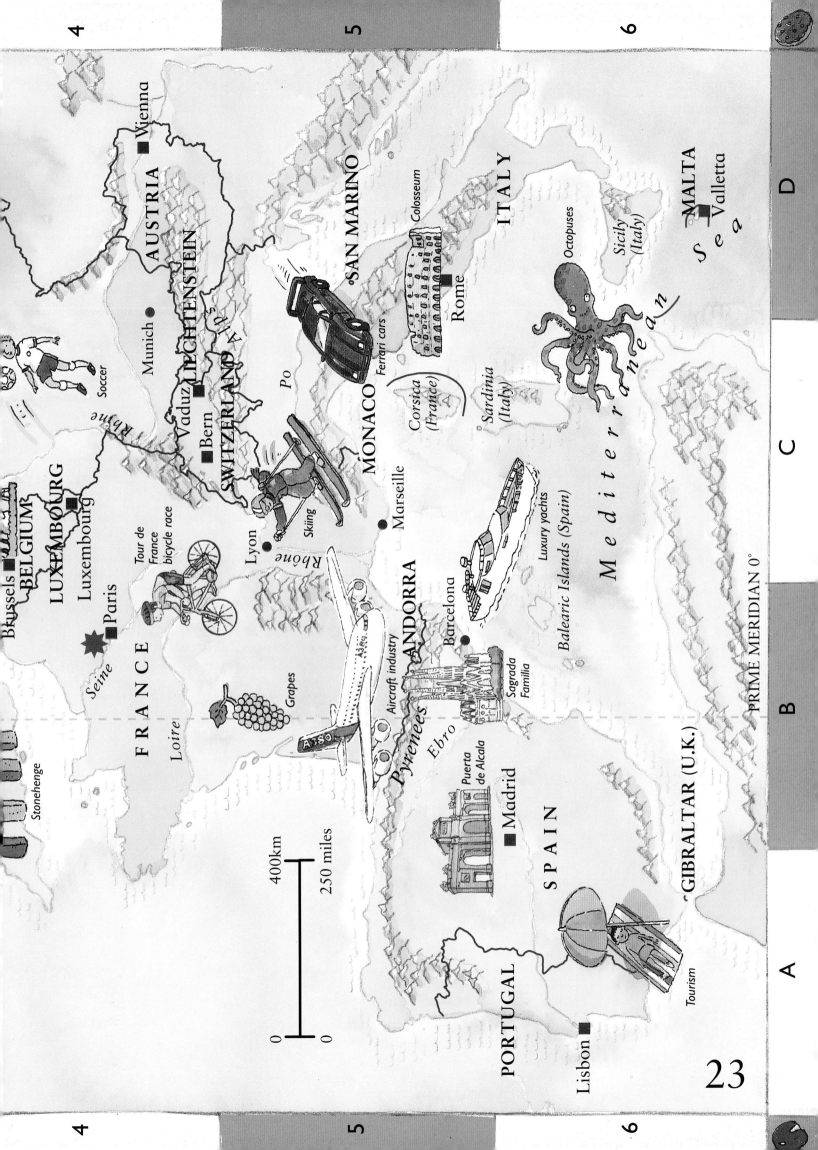

PORTUGAL

Lisbon

SPAIN

Madrid

Puerta
de Alcala

Tourism

GIBRALTAR (U.K.)

Ebro

Pyrenees

Sagrada
Familia

ANDORRA

Barcelona

Balearic Islands (Spain)

Luxury yachts

Mediterranean

Grapes

Aircraft industry

A380

A380

Loire

FRANCE

Seine

Paris

Stonehenge

BELGIUM
Brussels

LUXEMBOURG

Luxembourg

Tour de
France
bicycle race

Lyon

Rhône

Marseille

MONACO

Corsica
(France)

Sardinia
(Italy)

Octopuses

Sicily
(Italy)

S e a

MALTA

Valletta

PRIME MERIDIAN 0°

Rhône

Skiing

Bern

SWITZERLAND

Vaduz LIECHTENSTEIN

Munich

Soccer

Rhine

AUSTRIA

Vienna

Alps

Po

SAN MARINO

Ferrari cars

Colosseum

Rome

ITALY

0   400km

0   250 miles

23

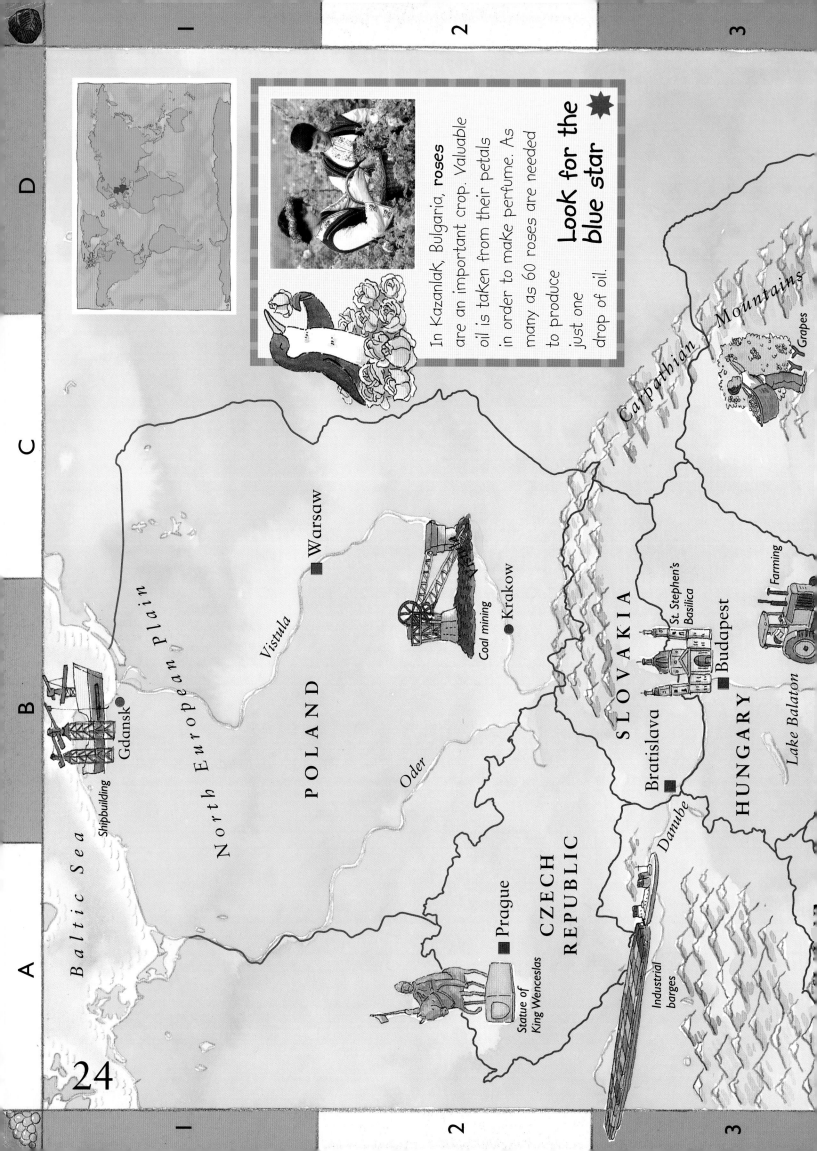

Look for the blue star ★

In Kazanlak, Bulgaria, **roses** are an important crop. Valuable oil is taken from their petals in order to make perfume. As many as 60 roses are needed to produce just one drop of oil.

Carpathian Mountains

Grapes

Baltic Sea

North European Plain

Shipbuilding

Gdansk

POLAND

Vistula

■ Warsaw

Coal mining

● Krakow

Oder

■ Prague

CZECH REPUBLIC

Statue of King Wenceslas

Danube

Industrial barges

SLOVAKIA

Bratislava

St. Stephen's Basilica

■ Budapest

HUNGARY

Lake Balaton

Farming

24

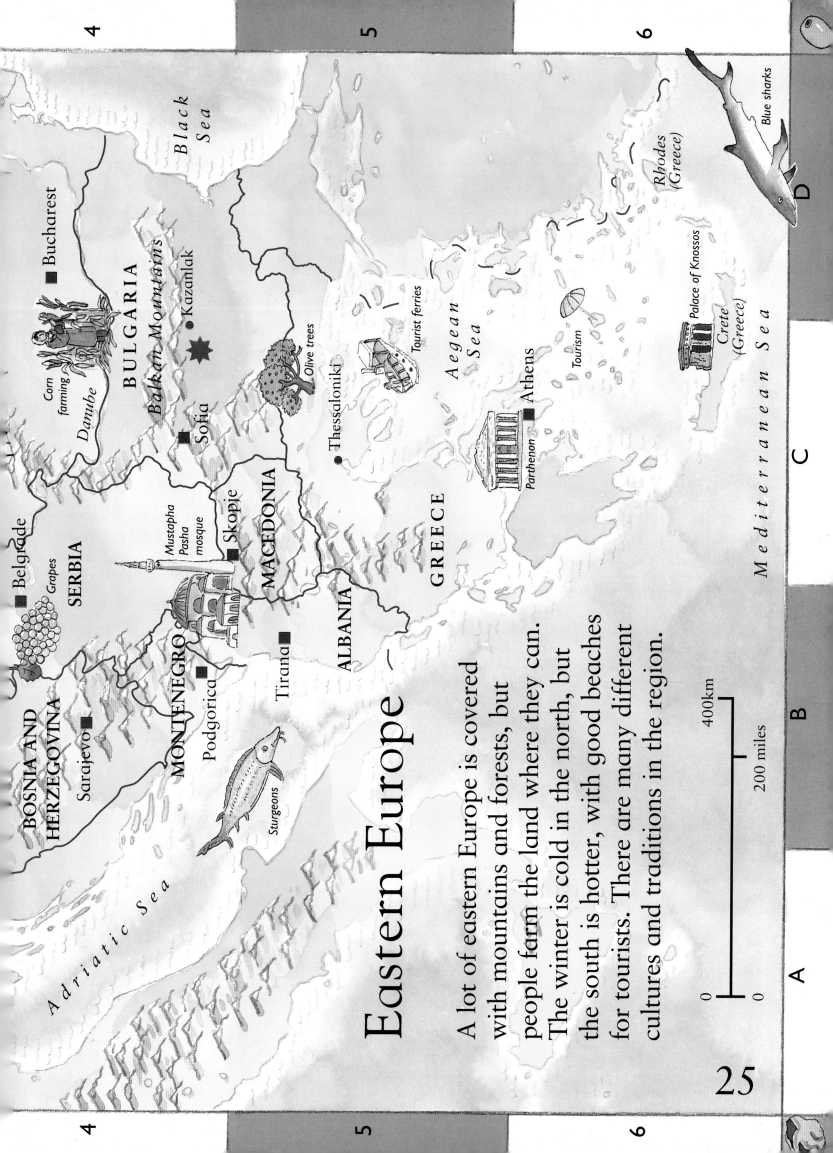

Eastern Europe

A lot of eastern Europe is covered with mountains and forests, but people farm the land where they can. The winter is cold in the north, but the south is hotter, with good beaches for tourists. There are many different cultures and traditions in the region.

BOSNIA AND HERZEGOVINA

Sarajevo

SERBIA

Belgrade

Grapes

MONTENEGRO

Podgorica

Sturgeons

Adriatic Sea

ALBANIA

Tirana

MACEDONIA

Skopje

Mustapha Pasha mosque

Balkan Mountains

BULGARIA

Sofia

Kazanlak

Danube

Corn farming

Bucharest

Black Sea

GREECE

Thessaloniki

Olive trees

Tourist ferries

Aegean Sea

Athens

Parthenon

Tourism

Mediterranean Sea

Palace of Knossos

Crete (Greece)

Rhodes (Greece)

Blue sharks

400km

200 miles

A   B   C   D

4   5   6

Russia and its neighbors

Russia is the biggest country in the world.
It stretches across the two continents
of Europe and Asia. Only one
fourth of Russia's land is
in Europe, but eight out
of ten Russians live in
this part of the country.
Many languages are
spoken in Russia.

Severnay Zemlya

Novaya Zemlya

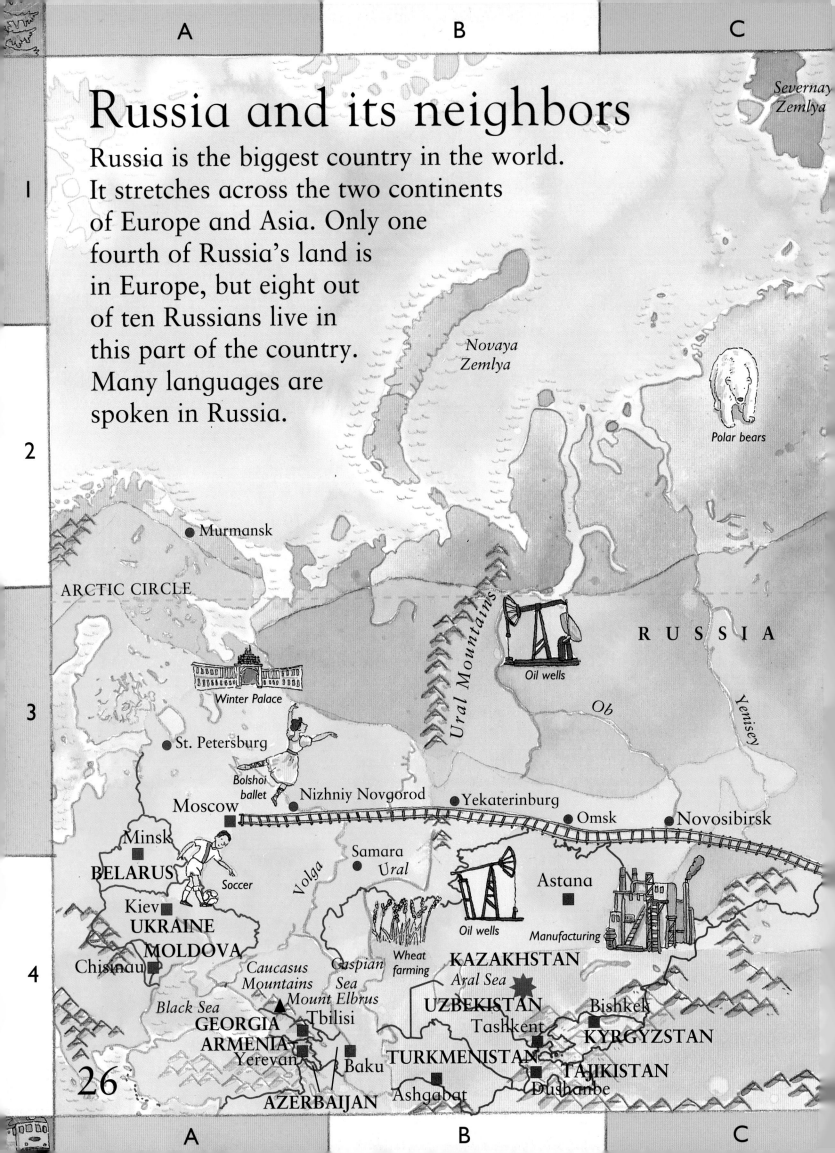

Polar bears

Murmansk

ARCTIC CIRCLE

RUSSIA

Ural Mountains

Oil wells

Ob

Yenisey

Winter Palace

Bolshoi ballet

St. Petersburg

Nizhniy Novgorod

Yekaterinburg

Omsk

Novosibirsk

Moscow

Minsk

BELARUS

Soccer

Samara

Volga

Ural

Astana

Manufacturing

Kiev

UKRAINE

MOLDOVA

Chisinau

Caucasus Mountains

Caspian Sea

Wheat farming

Oil wells

KAZAKHSTAN

Aral Sea

Black Sea

Mount Elbrus

Tbilisi

UZBEKISTAN

Tashkent

Bishkek

GEORGIA

ARMENIA

Yerevan

Baku

TURKMENISTAN

KYRGYZSTAN

TAJIKISTAN

Dushanbe

AZERBAIJAN

Ashgabat

26

1000km

500 miles

The **Baikonur cosmodrome** in Kazakhstan is the world's biggest spaceport. Many rockets are launched from there. **Look for the blue star** ✦

New Siberian Islands

Walrus

Polar cod

ymyr
insula

e forests

Lena

b   e   r   i   a

East Siberian Uplands

Gold mining

Diamond mining

● Yakutsk

Baikal

ns-Siberian Railroad

Amur

Tigers

Kamchatka Peninsula

Fishing

Sea of Okhotsk

Seals

Pacific Ocean

● Vladivostok

Istanbul

■ Ankara

TURKEY

Izmir

Black Se

Tourism

Sheep farming

■ Nicosia

CYPRUS   **SYRIA**

Beirut ■
LEBANON   ■ Damascus

M e d i t e r r a n e a n
S e a

ISRAEL
Jerusalem ■   ■ Amman

JORDAN

Bedouin
nomads

Southwestern Asia

Many countries in southwestern Asia
have hot, sandy deserts. The region is rich
in oil and natural gas. Crops can grow only
where there is water, in the lands near the
Mediterranean, Caspian, and Black seas.
Eastern Turkey and northern Iran have
mountains, plains, and grasslands,
which are cold in the winter.

Red Sea

M

The Great
Mosque

Mecca

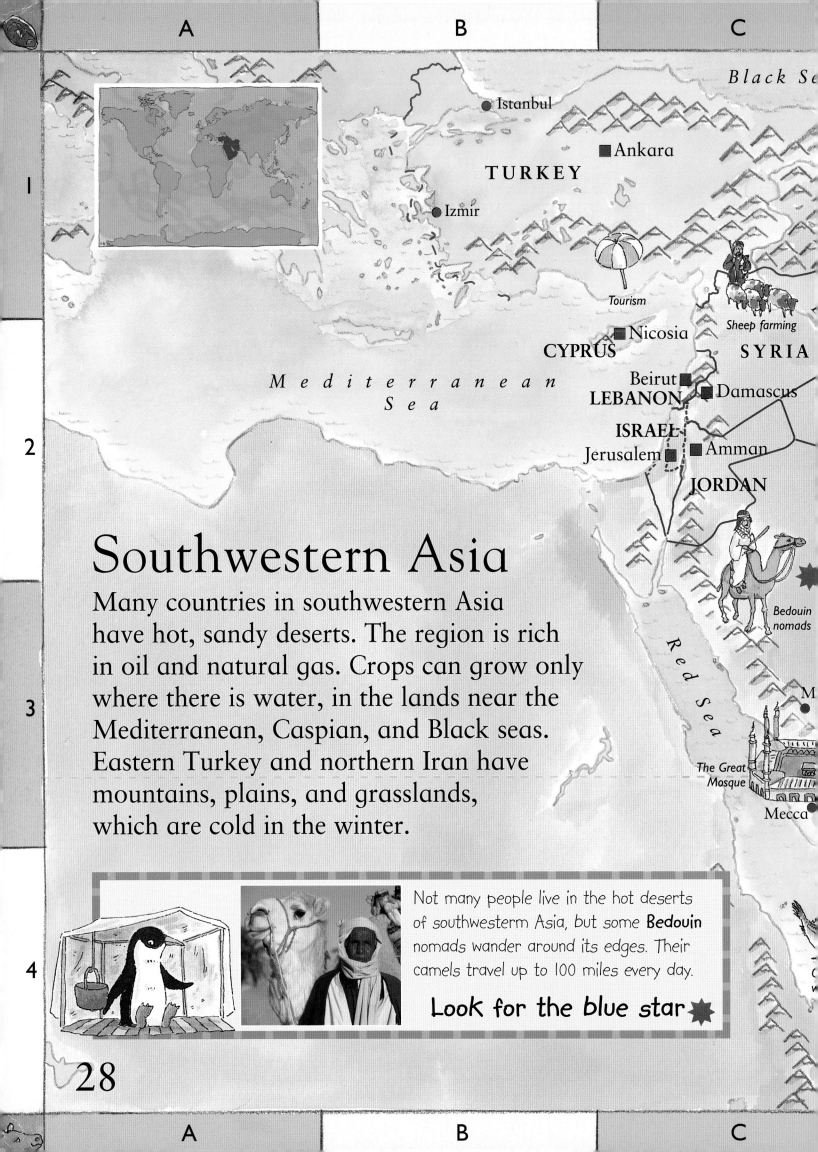

Not many people live in the hot deserts
of southwestern Asia, but some **Bedouin**
nomads wander around its edges. Their
camels travel up to 100 miles every day.

Look for the blue star ✦

28

0   800km

0   500 miles

I

Caspian Sea

• Tabriz

Oil rigs

Mashhad

Carpet making

Tehran

IRAN

Onagers

■ Baghdad

• Esfahan

2

IRAQ

Zagros Mountains

Basra

KUWAIT

■ Kuwait City

The Gulf

Oil refineries

Oil wells

BAHRAIN

OMAN

UDI ARABIA

■ Manama

Oil wells

QATAR

■ Doha

Riyadh ■

Abu Dhabi ■

3

UNITED ARAB
EMIRATES

■ Muscat

TROPIC OF CANCER

OMAN

rabian Desert

Dhows

*Ar Rub' al Khali
(Empty Quarter)*

*Arabian
Sea*

YEMEN

*Arabian
oryx*

*Orangespotted
trevallies*

4

• Sana

Dates

Gulf of Aden

• Aden

29

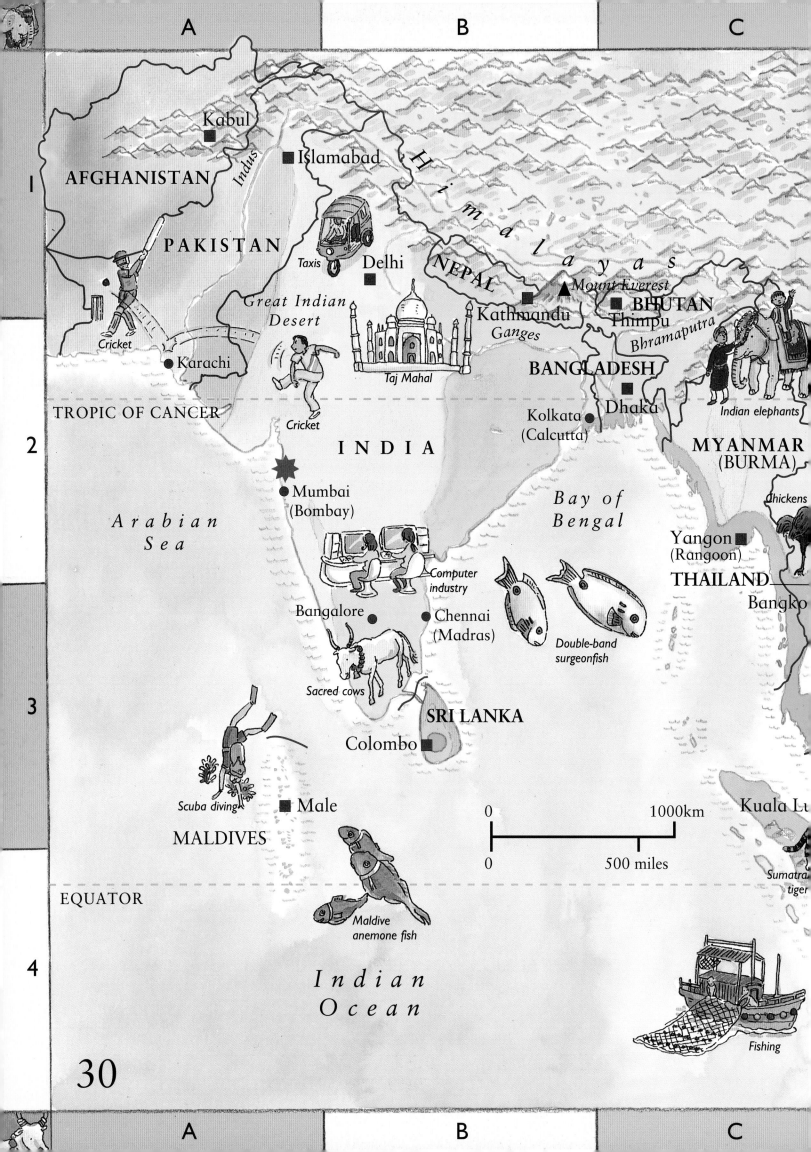

1

Kabul

Islamabad

Indus

AFGHANISTAN

PAKISTAN

H i m a l a y a s

Taxis

Delhi

NEPAL

▲ *Mount Everest*

Cricket

*Great Indian
Desert*

Kathmandu
Ganges

Thimpu

BHUTAN

Bhramaputra

Karachi

Taj Mahal

BANGLADESH

Indian elephants

TROPIC OF CANCER

Cricket

Dhaka

Kolkata
(Calcutta)

2

I N D I A

Chickens

**MYANMAR
(BURMA)**

*Arabian
Sea*

Mumbai
(Bombay)

*Bay of
Bengal*

Yangon
(Rangoon)

THAILAND

Bangko

Computer
industry

Bangalore

Chennai
(Madras)

*Double-band
surgeonfish*

Sacred cows

SRI LANKA

3

Colombo

Scuba diving

Male

Kuala Lu

MALDIVES

0   1000km

*Sumatra
tiger*

0   500 miles

*Maldive
anemone fish*

EQUATOR

4

*I n d i a n
O c e a n*

Fishing

30

outhern and southeastern Asia

e countries of this region are close to
e equator, so the weather is very hot. Dusty
ins stretch across India. Thick rain forests
w in Malaysia and Indonesia. Most people
m in small villages or work in big cities.
ong mountain range called the
malayas lies in the north.

NAM
Hanoi

ane

*South China
Sea*

Basket boats

ODIA

Rice

om

*Oil
rigs*

BRUNEI
Bandar Seri
Begawan

LAYSIA

GAPORE
pore

Orangutans

■ Manila

PHILIPPINES

The world's biggest
movie industry, **Bollywood**,
is based in Mumbai
(Bombay), India. Around
800 new movies are
made there every year.

Look for the
blue star ✶

I N D O N E S I A

Rain forests

■ Jakarta

■ Dili
EAST TIMOR

31

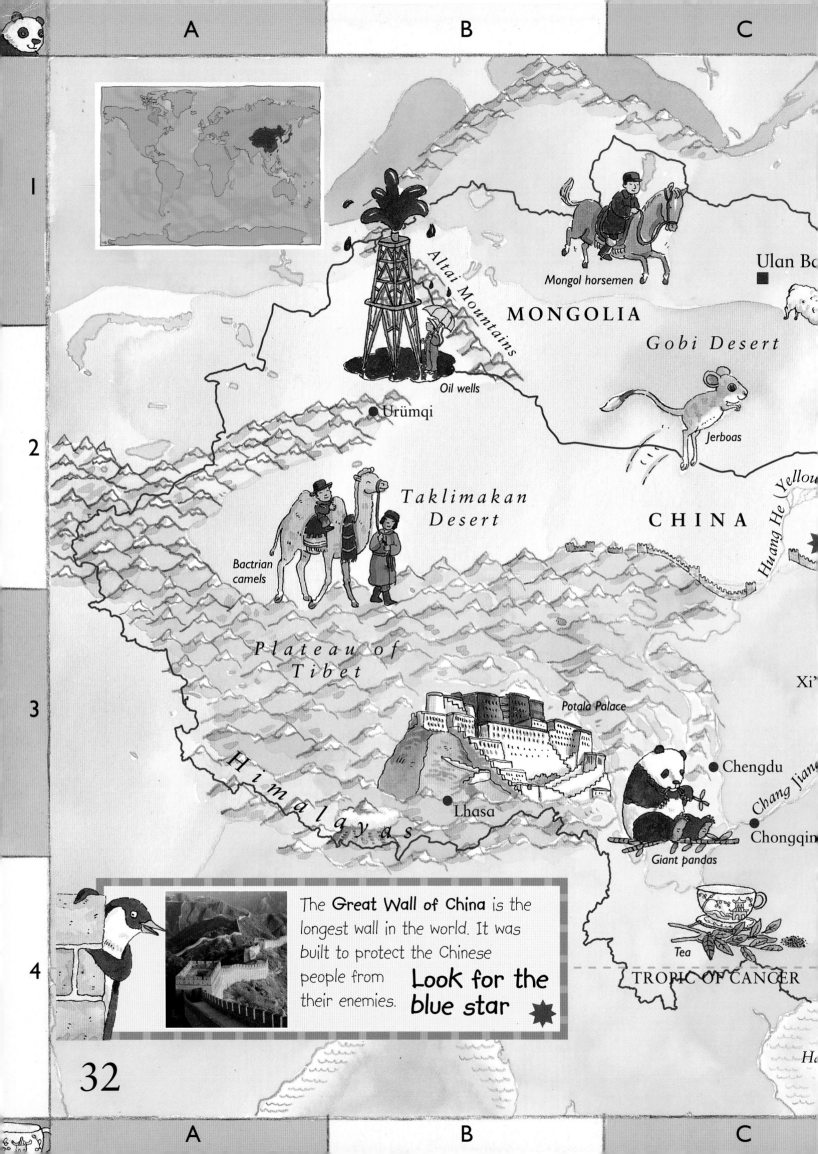

Altai Mountains

Mongol horsemen

MONGOLIA

Ulan Ba

Gobi Desert

Oil wells

Urümqi

Jerboas

Huang He (Yellow

Taklimakan Desert

CHINA

Bactrian camels

Plateau of Tibet

Potala Palace

Xi'

Chengdu

Himalayas

Chang Jian

Lhasa

Chongqin

Giant pandas

The **Great Wall of China** is the longest wall in the world. It was built to protect the Chinese people from their enemies. **Look for the blue star** ✵

Tea

TROPIC OF CANCER

Ha

32

0   1000km

0   500 miles

I

Great Khingan Range

Harbin

Manufacturing

2

Hokkaido

The Forbidden City

Shenyang

NORTH KOREA

Sea of Japan

Honshu

Squid

Shinkansen (Japanese bullet train)

jing

Tianjin

Pyongyang

Seoul

Bulguksa Temple

JAPAN

Mount Fuji

Tokyo

SOUTH KOREA

Nagoya

Terra-Cotta Army

Himeji Castle

Osaka

Chinese junks

Shikoku

3

Wuhan

Shanghai

East China Sea

Kyushu

China and Japan

More people live in China than anywhere else on Earth. Most settle in the east, where they can farm the land or work in cities. To the north is Mongolia, and to the east are North and South Korea, Taiwan, and Japan. Japan is made up of many islands. Most Japanese people live on the four main islands, Hokkaido, Honshu, Shikoku, and Kyushu, in very crowded cities.

Rice

Taipei

TAIWAN

4

angzhou

Hong Kong

th China Sea

33

PRIME MERIDIAN 0°

Atlantic Ocean

Mediterranean

Algiers

Tunis

TUNISIA

Tripoli

Rabat

Oil wells

Citrus fruits

MOROCCO

ALGERIA

LIBY

Berber people and camels

El Aaiún (Laayoune)

WESTERN SAHARA

S a h a r a

Ahaggar Mountains

Atlas Mountains

Tibest Mountai

MAURITANIA

Nouakchott

MALI

NIGER

Hippopotamuses

Cattle

Lake Chad

SENEGAL

Dakar

THE GAMBIA

Banjul

Bissau

GUINEA-BISSAU

Conakry

Freetown

SIERRA LEONE

Monrovia

LIBERIA

Peanuts

Diamonds

GUINEA

IVORY COAST

BURKINA FASO

Bamako

Ouagadougou

Niamey

Niger

Niger

N'Djamena

NIGERIA

Abuja

GHANA

TOGO

BENIN

Accra

Lomé

Porto Novo

Oil wells

Yamoussoukro

Street markets

EQUATOR

Fishing

34

0 ———— 1000k

0 ———— 500 miles

Northern Africa

The Sahara is the world's biggest desert. It stretches across all of northern Africa. Most people live south of the Sahara or near the coast. The world's longest river, the Nile, flows from central Africa through Egypt to the Mediterranean Sea.

TROPIC OF CANCER

EGYPT

Tutankhamen's funerary mask

Lake Nasser

scorpions

Cotton

Nile

Red Sea

■ Cairo

Crocodiles

ERITREA

■ Khartoum   ■ Asmara

SUDAN

Ethiopian Highlands

DJIBOUTI

■ Addis Ababa

ETHIOPIA

SOMALIA

■ Mogadishu

Starry triggerfish

Indian Ocean

The **pyramids**, near Cairo in Egypt, were built more than 4,000 years ago. They are the largest stone buildings in the world. **Look for the blue star** ✶

1

2

3

4

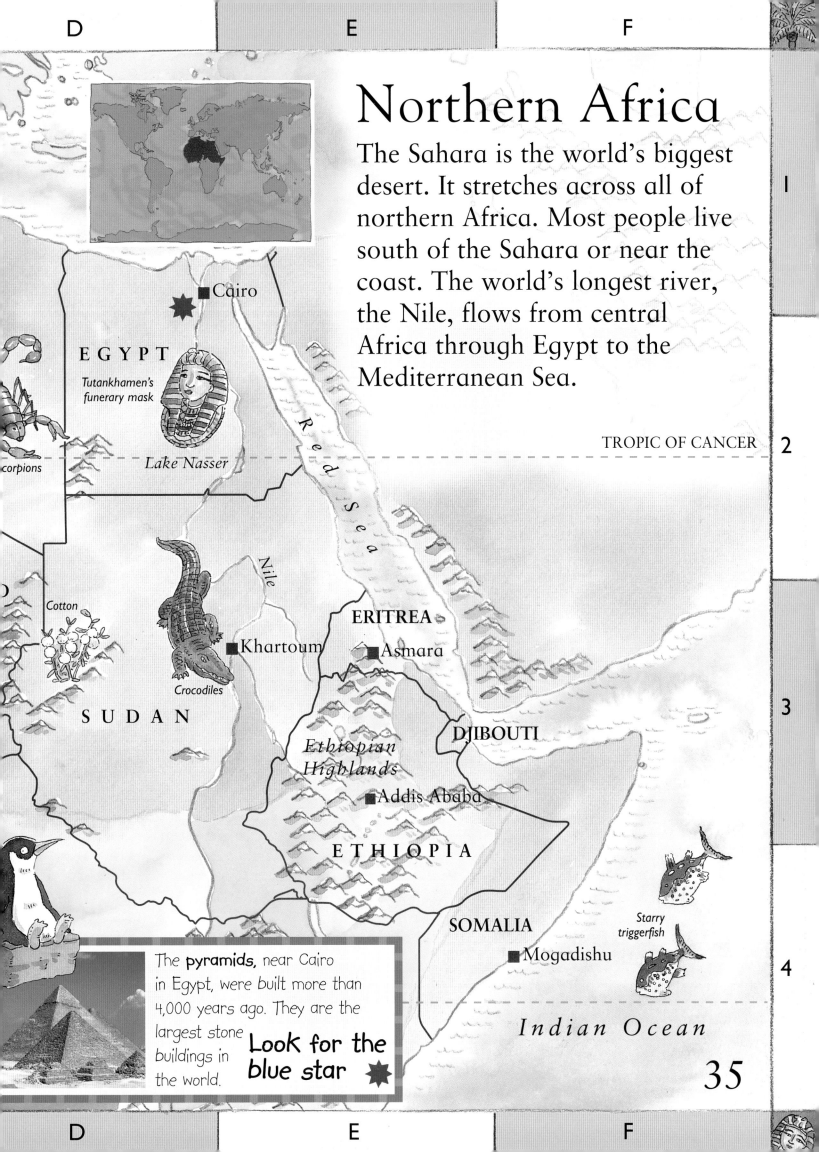

Southern Africa

Countries on the east coast of Africa, such as Kenya, are famous for the wildlife on their flat grasslands. Lions, elephants, and giraffes all live on the savanna. To the west of Africa the Congo river runs through a thick rain forest. The huge Kalahari Desert is at the heart of southern Africa.

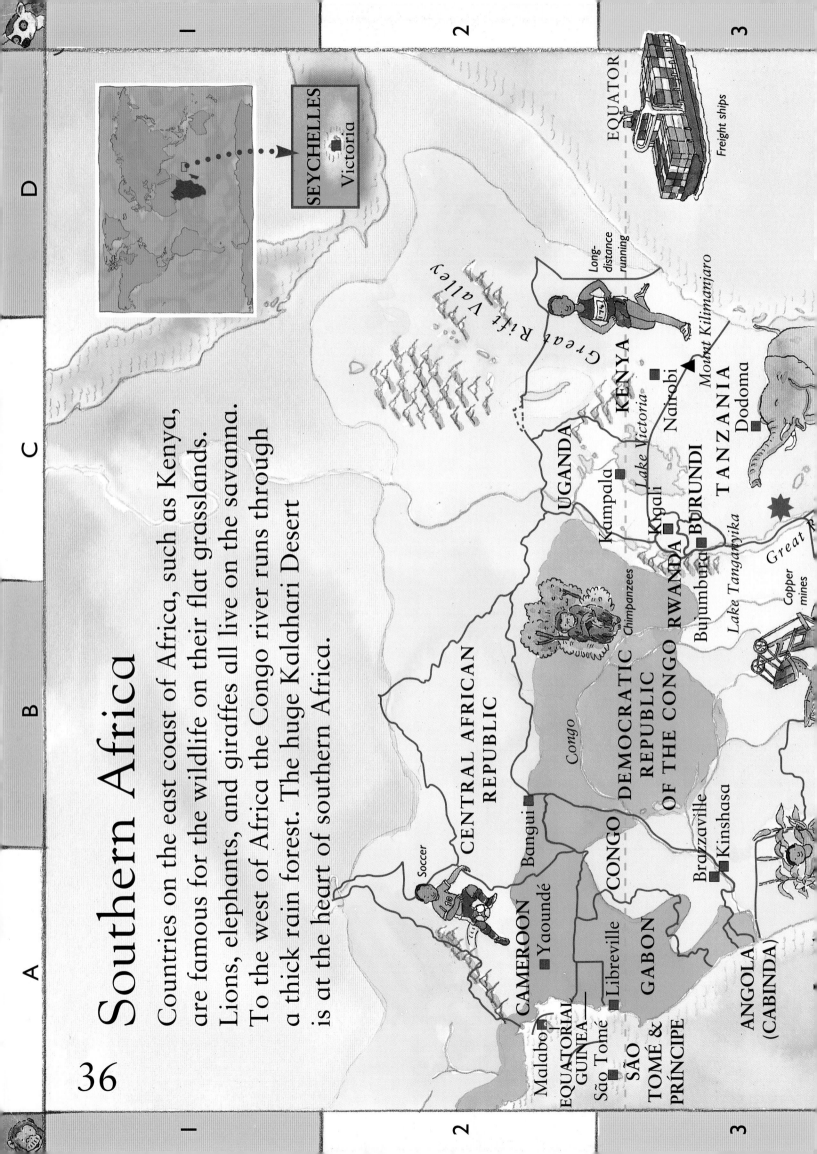

SEYCHELLES
Victoria

A   B   C   D

1   2   3

EQUATOR

Freight ships

Long-distance running

Great Rift Valley

KENYA
Nairobi
Lake Victoria

Mount Kilimanjaro

TANZANIA
Dodoma

UGANDA
Kampala

RWANDA
Kigali

BURUNDI
Bujumbura

Lake Tanganyika

Copper mines

Great R

CENTRAL AFRICAN REPUBLIC

Chimpanzees

Congo

DEMOCRATIC REPUBLIC OF THE CONGO

CONGO

Brazzaville
Kinshasa

Soccer

CAMEROON
Yaoundé

Bangui

Libreville

GABON

Malabo
EQUATORIAL GUINEA
São Tomé
SÃO TOMÉ & PRÍNCIPE

ANGOLA
(CABINDA)

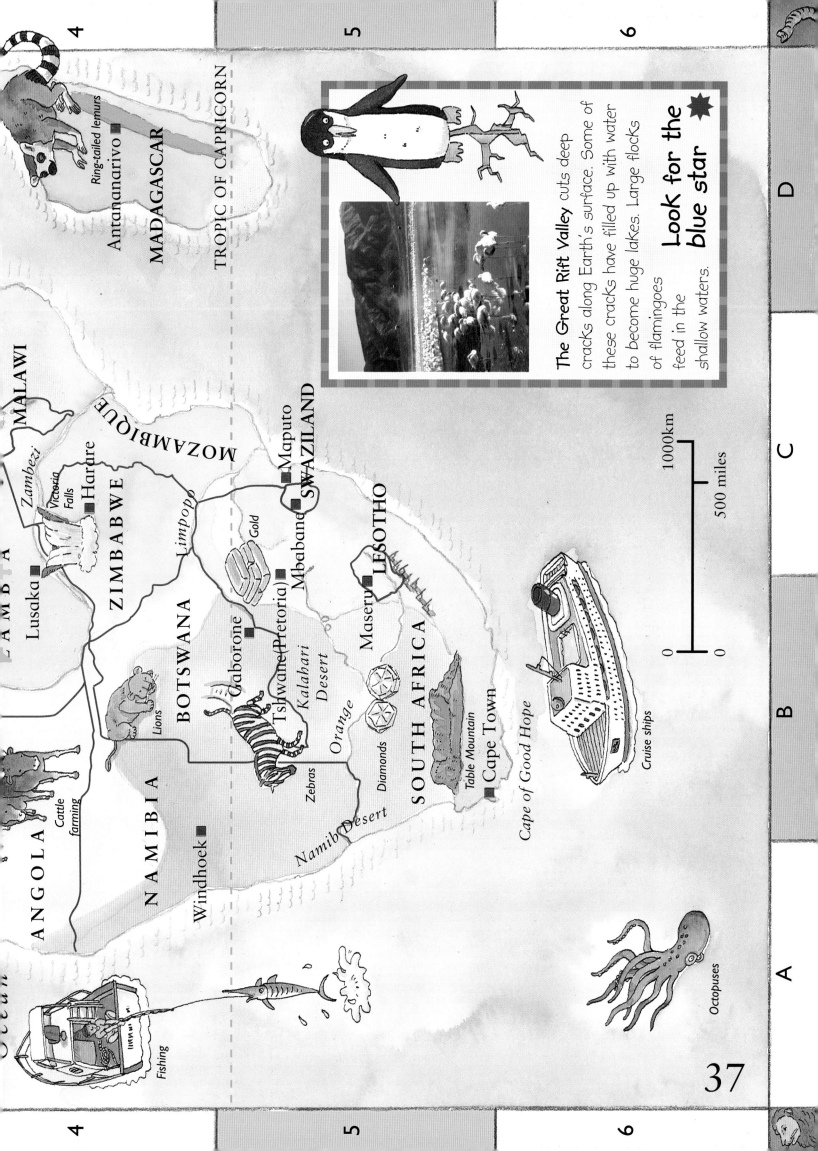

The Great Rift Valley cuts deep cracks along Earth's surface. Some of these cracks have filled up with water to become huge lakes. Large flocks of flamingoes feed in the shallow waters.

★ Look for the **blue star**

Ring-tailed lemurs

Antananarivo

MADAGASCAR

TROPIC OF CAPRICORN

MALAWI

Lusaka

Zambezi

Victoria Falls

Harare

ZIMBABWE

MOZAMBIQUE

Maputo

SWAZILAND

Mbabane

Gold

Limpopo

BOTSWANA

Gaborone

Tshwane (Pretoria)

Kalahari Desert

Maseru

LESOTHO

Lions

Orange

Zebras

Diamonds

SOUTH AFRICA

NAMIBIA

Windhoek

Namib Desert

Table Mountain

Cape Town

Cape of Good Hope

Cruise ships

ANGOLA

Cattle farming

Fishing

Octopuses

1000km

500 miles

0

0

4

5

6

A

B

C

D

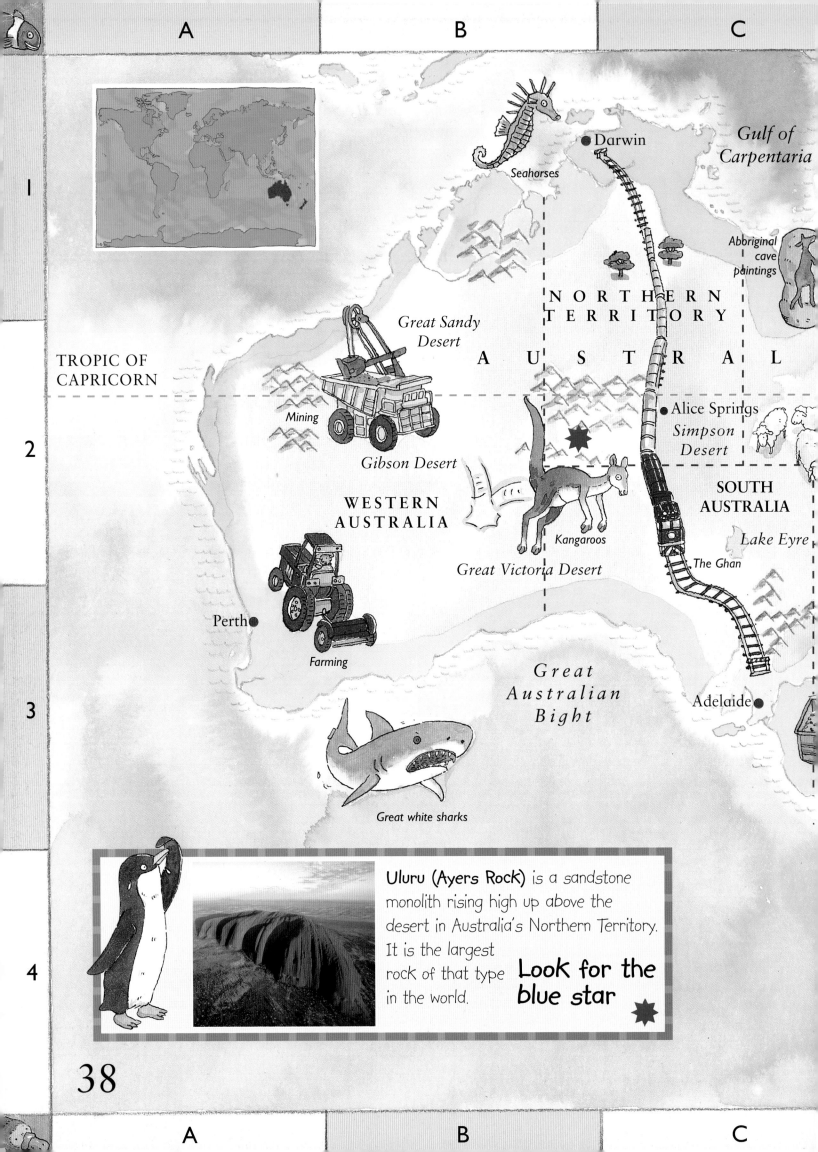

I

TROPIC OF
CAPRICORN

2

3

4

Seahorses

● Darwin

*Gulf of
Carpentaria*

Abriginal
cave
paintings

N O R T H E R N
T E R R I T O R Y
A U S T R A L

*Great Sandy
Desert*

Mining

Gibson Desert

WESTERN
AUSTRALIA

Kangaroos

Great Victoria Desert

● Alice Springs
*Simpson
Desert*

SOUTH
AUSTRALIA

Lake Eyre

The Ghan

Perth ●

Farming

*Great
Australian
Bight*

Adelaide ●

Great white sharks

Uluru (Ayers Rock) is a sandstone
monolith rising high up above the
desert in Australia's Northern Territory.
It is the largest
rock of that type
in the world.

**Look for the
blue star** ✦

1

Australia and New Zealand

Australia is the only country that is also a continent. In the middle there are many deserts. In northern Australia there are tropical rain forests. Most Australian people live in cities by the sea.

New Zealand is 620 miles away from Australia. It is a land of mountains and glaciers. Like Australia, it has many sheep and cattle farms.

Coral Sea

Clown fish

iding Range

ENSLAND   ● Brisbane

Duck-billed platypuses

W SOUTH WALES

Sydney ●   Sydney Opera House

■ Canberra
AUSTRALIAN CAPITAL
TERRITORY

ay

RIA
ourne

Surfing

trait

Tasmanian devils

Tasman Sea

● Hobart

SMANIA

1000km

500 miles

Red snappers

Rugby

Pacific Ocean

NORTH ISLAND

NEW
ZEALAND

● Auckland

● Hamilton

Lake Taupo

■ Wellington

Kiwi birds

SOUTH ISLAND

Mount Cook ▲   *Southern Alps*

● Christchurch

Fishing

● Dunedin

Yellowfin tuna

2

3

4

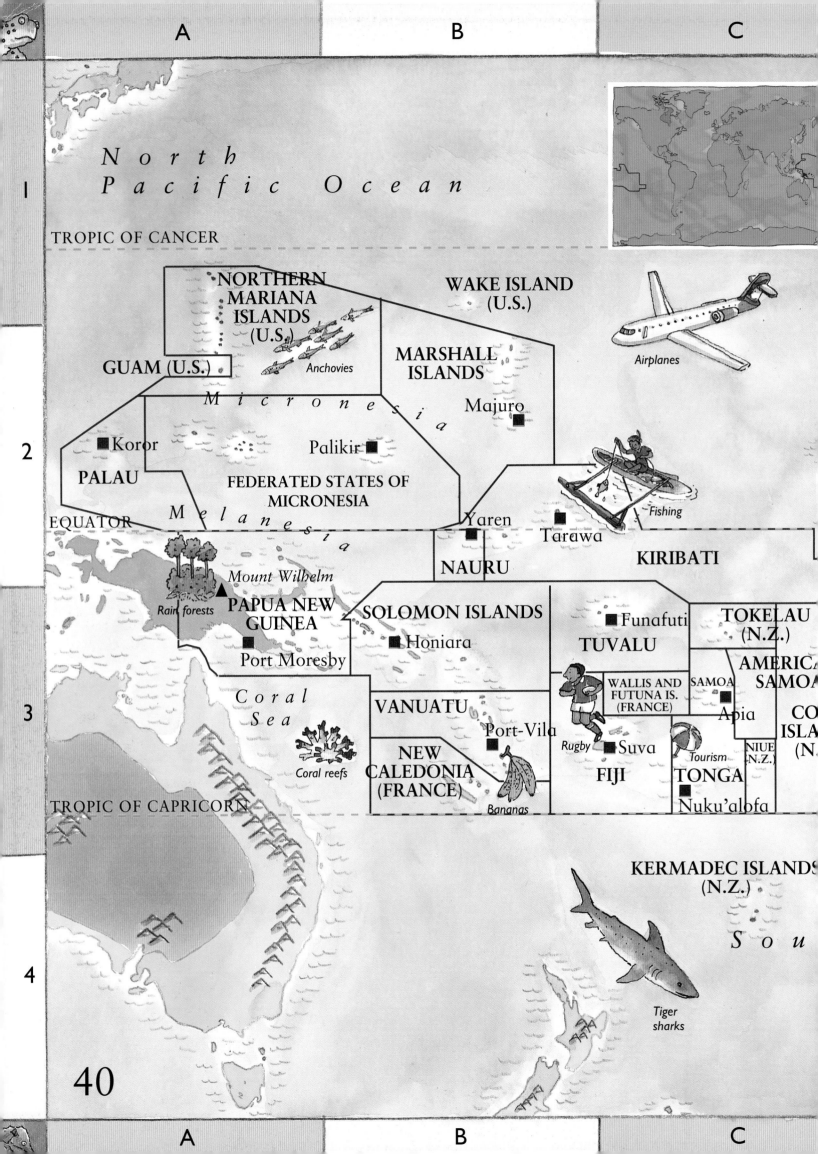

North Pacific Ocean

TROPIC OF CANCER

NORTHERN MARIANA ISLANDS (U.S.)

Anchovies

WAKE ISLAND (U.S.)

GUAM (U.S.)

M i c r o n e s i a

MARSHALL ISLANDS

Majuro

Airplanes

Koror

Palikir

PALAU

FEDERATED STATES OF MICRONESIA

M e l a n e s i a

EQUATOR

Yaren

Tarawa

Fishing

KIRIBATI

NAURU

Mount Wilhelm

PAPUA NEW GUINEA

Rain forests

SOLOMON ISLANDS

Honiara

Funafuti

TOKELAU (N.Z.)

TUVALU

AMERICAN SAMOA

Port Moresby

Coral Sea

VANUATU

Port-Vila

Rugby

WALLIS AND FUTUNA IS. (FRANCE)

SAMOA

Apia

CO ISLANDS (N.

Coral reefs

NEW CALEDONIA (FRANCE)

Suva

Tourism

NIUE (N.Z.)

TROPIC OF CAPRICORN

Bananas

FIJI

TONGA

Nuku'alofa

KERMADEC ISLANDS (N.Z.)

S o u

Tiger sharks

40

1
2
3
4

he Pacific islands

here are thousands of islands
the Pacific Ocean. All of these
ands, together with Australia,
ew Zealand, and Papua New
uinea, make up a region called Oceania.
any Pacific islanders live in communities
at have little contact with the rest of
e world. Some of their traditions have
t changed for hundreds of years.

More than 1,000 years ago,
settlers on Easter Island
carved these huge **heads**
out of volcanic rock. The
statues may represent
the island's great chiefs.

**Look for the
blue star**

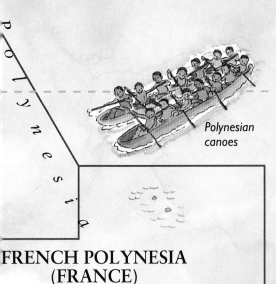

*Polynesian
canoes*

**GALÁPAGOS ISLANDS
(ECUADOR)**

Sea turtles

Cruise ships

**FRENCH POLYNESIA
(FRANCE)**

Tahiti

*Long-nosed
seahorses*

**PITCAIRN
ISLANDS
(U.K.)**

TROPIC OF CAPRICORN

 **EASTER ISLAND
(CHILE)**

acific   Ocean

0 ————— 1000km

0 ————— 500 miles

41

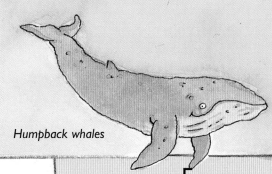

Humpback whales

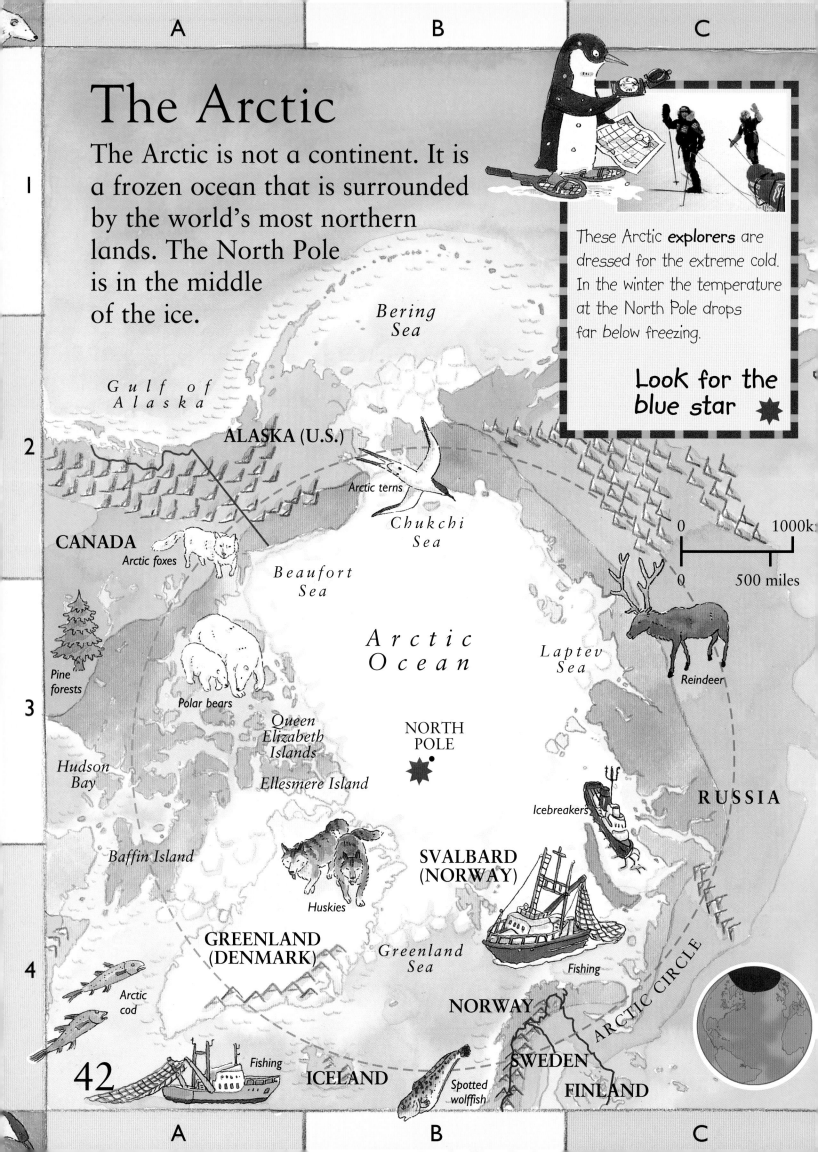

The Arctic

The Arctic is not a continent. It is a frozen ocean that is surrounded by the world's most northern lands. The North Pole is in the middle of the ice.

These Arctic **explorers** are dressed for the extreme cold. In the winter the temperature at the North Pole drops far below freezing.

Look for the blue star ✴

Bering Sea

Gulf of Alaska

ALASKA (U.S.)

Arctic terns

Chukchi Sea

0   1000k

0   500 miles

CANADA

Arctic foxes

Beaufort Sea

Arctic Ocean

Laptev Sea

Reindeer

Pine forests

Polar bears

Queen Elizabeth Islands

NORTH POLE
✴

Hudson Bay

Ellesmere Island

Icebreakers

RUSSIA

Baffin Island

Huskies

SVALBARD (NORWAY)

GREENLAND (DENMARK)

Greenland Sea

Fishing

Arctic cod

NORWAY

ARCTIC CIRCLE

42

Fishing

ICELAND

Spotted wolffish

SWEDEN

FINLAND

Antarctica

Antarctica is the world's most remote continent. Only scientists live here— in the coldest and windiest place on Earth. Almost all of Antarctica is covered with ice. The South Pole is in the middle of Antarctica.

0 1000km

0 500 miles

Antarctica has 90 percent of all of the world's ice. The biggest **iceberg** that has been spotted was found in the Antarctic and was bigger than the country of Belgium.

Look for the blue star ✴

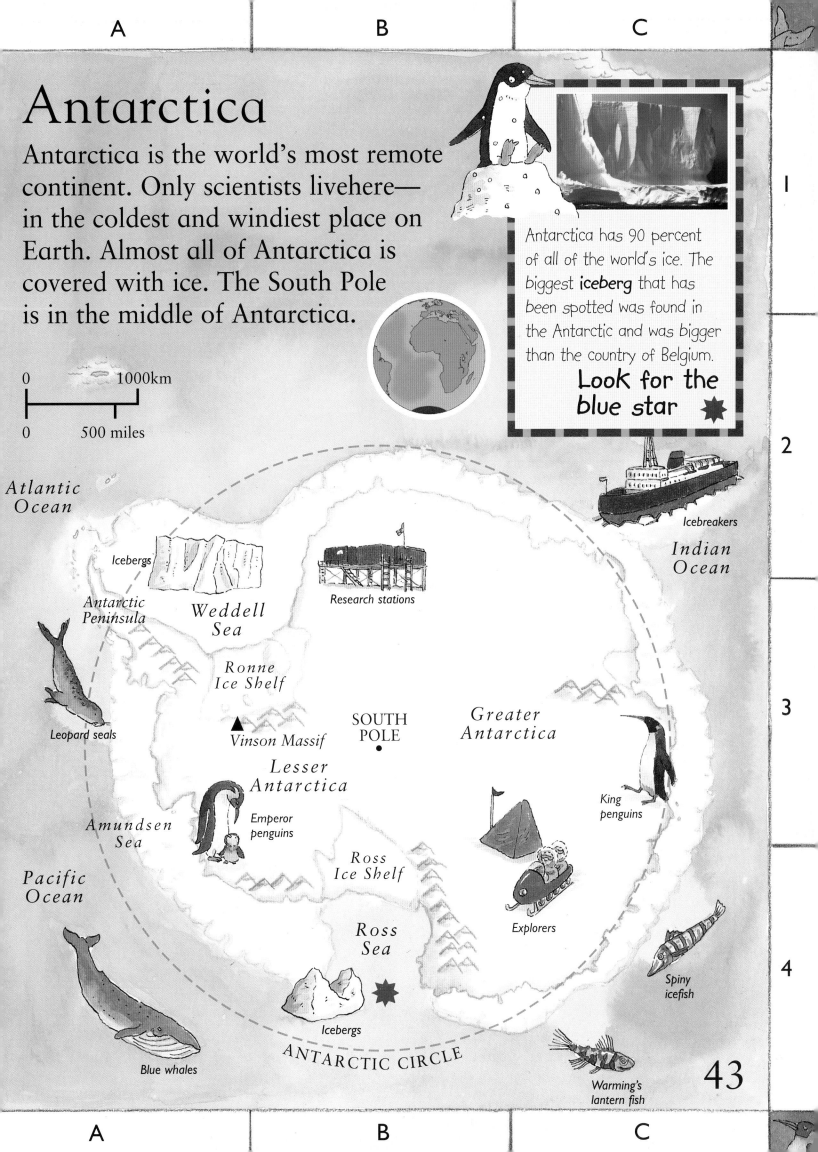

Atlantic Ocean

Icebergs

Antarctic Peninsula

Weddell Sea

Research stations

Icebreakers

Indian Ocean

Ronne Ice Shelf

SOUTH POLE

Greater Antarctica

▲ *Vinson Massif*

Leopard seals

Lesser Antarctica

Emperor penguins

King penguins

Amundsen Sea

Ross Ice Shelf

Pacific Ocean

Explorers

Ross Sea

Spiny icefish

Icebergs

✴

ANTARCTIC CIRCLE

Blue whales

Warming's lantern fish

43

ARCTIC CIRCLE

Fish

Deep-sea
submersibles

*Blue
whales*

Car ferries

TROPIC OF CANCER

Cruise ships

Oil rigs

*Caribbean
Sea*

Scuba
diving

*Atlantic
Ocean*

EQUATOR

*Pacific
Ocean*

Fishing

Freight
ships

TROPIC OF CAPRICORN

Fishing

The oceans

Seen from space, Earth looks
blue. This is because almost three
fourths of the planet is covered
with water. Earth has four major
oceans, the Pacific, Atlantic, Indian,
and Arctic. The Pacific is the
biggest of these oceans.

Oil rigs

Factory
fishing ships

Icebergs

PRIM
MERIDIA

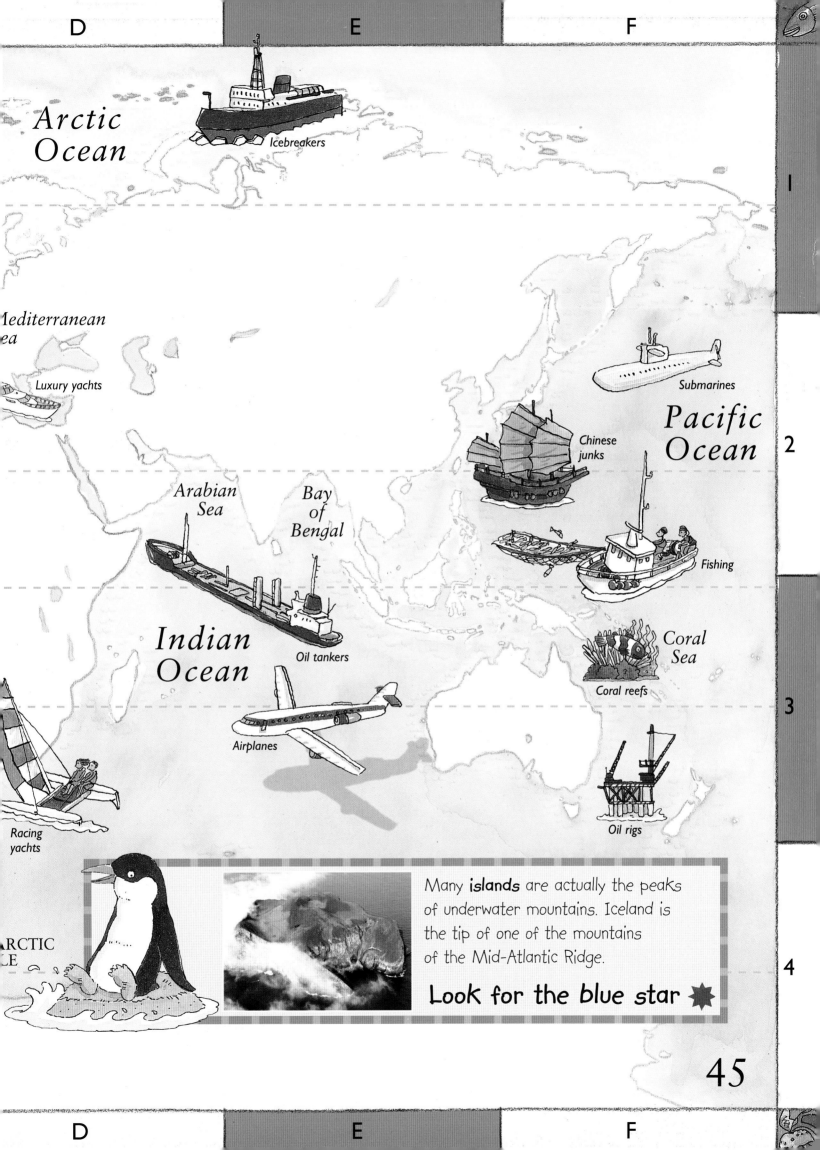

Arctic Ocean

Icebreakers

Mediterranean Sea

Luxury yachts

Arabian Sea

Bay of Bengal

Indian Ocean

Oil tankers

Airplanes

Racing yachts

Submarines

Pacific Ocean

Chinese junks

Fishing

Coral Sea

Coral reefs

Oil rigs

ARCTIC CIRCLE

Many **islands** are actually the peaks of underwater mountains. Iceland is the tip of one of the mountains of the Mid-Atlantic Ridge.

Look for the blue star ✦

45

Index